Ekklesia
Empowered and Deployed

This booklet is about the purpose and the activation of the true and mobile Church of Jesus Christ.

Ron Hamilton

Endorsements

"Ron Hamilton is passionate about the church. He always has been. I will never forget our first meeting at Robert's Barbecue in North Charleston, SC. I wanted to gauge his interest in joining me in a new adventure called Seacoast Church. He wasn't just interested, he was passionate about the possibilities. Thirty-two years later we are still living out the ideas that we scribbled on a napkin that day.

Now Ron has published his passion in this book called *Ekklesia: Empowered and Deployed* so that generations will be able to experience the power of what the church can be.

Ron has always been passionate about the potential of the Kingdom of God on Earth. My life has certainly been marked by it. I hope yours will be too."

--Greg Surratt

Greg is the founding pastor of Seacoast Church, one of the early adopters of the multi-site model. Located in Mt Pleasant, South Carolina, Seacoast has been recognized by various media as an innovative and influential thought leader in future strategies for church growth and development. Greg is the president and founding board member of the Association of Related Churches (ARC), a church-planting network that has given birth to 900+ churches in the last 14 years. Greg and his wife Debbie have 4 children, 14 grandchildren and enjoy reading, photography, fishing, golfing, and rooting for the Cubs, Broncos and Gamecocks.

"I loved *Ekklesia: Empowered and Deployed*! Ron Hamilton's clear understanding of the Ekklesia, in the context of real practical, kingdom deployment, is something I can recommend to anyone and everyone. Get this reformation paradigm added to your revival paradigm."

--Johnny Enlow

Johnny Enlow is a father to 5, grandfather, social reformer, international speaker, spiritual mentor, and author of *The Seven Mountain Prophecy, The Seven Mountain Mantle, Rainbow God, The Seven Mountain Renaissance,* and *Becoming A Superhero*. He and his wife Elizabeth as a team are focused on awakening individuals to their call to provide practical solutions from the heart of God for every problem in society-until the real God of all of life is displayed in the 7 primary areas of culture in all nations: Media, Arts and Entertainment, Government, Family, Religion, Economy, and Education.

The Church as a Transformational Agency

What comes to mind when you hear the word "church"? For a lot of us, it has been a building with an address or maybe a religious organization that provides many activities and charitable works. As far as church experiences, one of the most amazing revolutions over the last 30 years has been the way churches have created accessible on-ramps for more people to experience church both on-site and online. Surprisingly though, when Jesus decided to describe the group of people that would carry out His purpose on the earth, He did not choose a word connected with current religious experiences.

When Jesus first introduced the word "church" in Matthew 16:18, He did not use the word for temple, synagogue, or tabernacle-- all religious institutions of the time. When He said, "I will build my church," He chose the secular Greek word, "ecclesia." Strong's concordance defines ecclesia from the greek word, ἐκκλησία, ἐκκλεσιας, ἡ (from ἔκκλητος called out or forth, and this from ἐκκαλέω); properly, as **a gathering of citizens called out from their homes into some public place; an assembly**. Only later did Christian translators define it as a gathering of believers for worship. Imagine the shock on the faces of those surrounding Him when He used a word that had no religious connotation at all! Instead, He used a word that described an institution whose primary function was operating in secular marketplaces in a governmental capacity.

Ecclesia, as an institution, was one of the three main entities of that time. The other two, the temple and synagogue, were buildings that housed religious activities; however ecclesia was secular and could assemble anywhere. The Romans adapted the concept of ecclesia from the Greeks, who created it as a ruling assembly of citizens to govern its city-states. The highest level of ecclesia in Rome was the Roman Senate: members would legislate and conduct government business on behalf of the Emperor. Rome also empowered loyal, local citizens to gather and legislate locally as well. They did so with the Emperor's agenda and on his behalf: for the good of the empire. Ecclesia groups of citizens were formed throughout the Roman Empire to legislate governmental business for Rome. We find the word ecclesia mentioned 5 times in Acts 19 describing citizens so gathered.

Now think about that in context with the words of Jesus! When the moment came to introduce His transformational agency on the earth, Jesus rejected the two Jewish religious institutions of the day, both of which needed specific buildings to function. Instead, He announced that He would build His ecclesia, or in Hebrew-- ekklesia. In selecting a term used to describe a group of citizens with governmental responsibility, He made the radical distinction that His chosen citizens were mobile and could meet outside of the confines of a building.

His disciples and followers understood the concept of the Roman ecclesia. I believe it was the only entity understood in that day that could describe the purpose and intent He had for His kingdom. It is important to note that Jesus did not come as a religious figure; He came as a King with the government of His nation on His shoulders that would know no end (Isaiah 9:6-7).

As we begin to understand the ramifications of the entity of ecclesia that Jesus described and its power to transform society, we must also pause to consider how best ecclesia functions in this legislative capacity to bring the reality of Kingdom government on earth. In Matthew 16:19, Jesus follows up His ecclesia announcement with this amazing promise: "I will give you the keys to the kingdom of heaven; and whatever you bind on earth shall be bound in heaven and whatever you loose on earth shall have been loosed in heaven." This statement begins to reveal the power that ecclesia has to agree with and mirror what is in heaven. Jesus repeats this same promise in Matthew 18:18. In the two verses that follow, He then adds incredible insight into how ecclesia will best accomplish this legislative function of agreeing with heaven's government: "Again I say to you, if two of you agree on Earth about anything that they may ask, it shall be done for them by my Father who is in heaven. For where two or three have gathered together in my name, I am there in their midst" (Matthew 18:19-20).

I believe that Jesus is giving us the secret of ecclesia's power: the power of agreement, which is done best in smaller groups! I have been privileged to be a part of one of the most life-giving churches of our day that, through our large weekend gatherings, has brought multiple thousands through the door of the Kingdom. When it comes to experiencing the presence of God, there is undeniable value that comes from gathering in corporate worship and teaching that is hard to reproduce in small groups. However, I believe we have to pay attention to the secret Jesus reveals here about how His powerful ecclesia best functions: in smaller groups of agreement to bring the reality of heaven into our world and as we will see, through our assignments. So come with me as we explore both the functionality and the implications for the Kingdom of God's citizens to be ecclesia, or Ekklesia, the transforming entity that Jesus declared He would build.

The Kingdom of God

Jesus Reestablishes the Kingdom
Jesus came in the fullness of time to re-establish the Kingdom of God on the earth. He came to RE-establish it because the Kingdom of God had already been introduced on the earth through Adam and Eve. First, let's address why Earth was formed and get a view of God's purpose in creating mankind and the mandate He gave us from the beginning.

Psalm 10:16 declares that the Lord is King forever and ever. Psalm 47:7 declares that God is the King of all the earth. King Nebuchadnezzar in Daniel 4:37 calls God the "King of Heaven."

Kings have domains, territories that belong to them; therefore, Kingdom means the *King's Domain*. Since God is King, He has always had a kingdom. Heaven is a real place and is the spiritual domain where God rules. It is from here that He created all things. God, Who is love, first created mankind to share that love with us and second, to entrust us to bring the culture of His Kingdom to His new territory.

Think of earthly kings-- they want sons and daughters to rule their territory with their DNA and to operate on the principles established by their royal house. They send trusted envoys to their colonies to "colonize" or bring the nature and culture of the kingdom to the new territory. This is similar to what God did when He created Earth and then created man. Though colonization is sometimes seen as a negative act of invading culture into an indigenous population, this is instead God sending spiritual sons and daughters to His created colony called Earth, bringing the culture of His amazing Kingdom.

In light of this understanding, Genesis 1:26-27 takes on new significance and highlights the purpose and plan of God for us: "Then God said, 'Let Us make man in Our image, according to Our likeness; let them have dominion over the fish of the sea, over the birds of the air, and over the cattle, over all the earth and over every creeping thing that creeps on the earth.' So God created man in His own image; in the image of God He created him; male and female He created them" (NKJV).

Adam and Eve were created in His image and likeness for His purpose: to colonize Earth with the reality of Heaven. It is important to see they were made with both His image and likeness. His image brings the who of God: His nature, character, and identity. His likeness carries more of the how of God: His functionality and His ways. What is key here is that the first gift God gave man was His image and likeness, but the first mandate and assignment He gave them was dominion.

God's plan was always His unseen Spirit inside physical bodies on the earth, His territory. They would have the Kingdom *in them* because they were created with God the King *in them*. They were made spiritual children of God, sons and daughters to be His representatives on the earth. His indwelling presence in them brought what I will tag as CCC: constant communication and connection with the will, mind, intent, and purposes of God and Heaven. Because of this, we are co-regents sent to rule and manage the earth as He would, bringing both mankind and the earth into their full creative purpose.

This relationship between the Spirit of God and Adam and Eve made God's Spirit the key component of bringing the Kingdom of Heaven on the earth. This is why the decision, recorded in Genesis 3, that Adam and Eve made to rebel against the King and His purpose was so tragic. The lost connection with the Spirit of God would render mankind an empty envoy of Heaven, no longer knowing the will or mind of the King of Heaven for the earth. In effect, Adam not only lost his relationship with his heavenly Father, but he lost a kingdom. He became an ambassador without a government, a citizen without a country, a king without a kingdom, and a ruler without a domain.

The good news is that when Jesus came to the earth, He came to not only bring the reality of the Kingdom back to Earth but to also model and re-establish the CCC, the constant communication and connection with the Spirit of God that man so desperately needed to fulfill his mandate to bring God's Kingdom on Earth.

Now we see why Jesus came proclaiming, as in Matthew 4:17, "Repent, for the Kingdom of heaven is here." Repent is the Greek word, metanoia, and calls for a brand new way of thinking. Jesus knew that the only way we would receive this Kingdom was through a new mindset. He came as the second Adam to recover the authority the first Adam lost and to restore the dominion purpose given to the first humans in Genesis 1:26-27, the mandate that Adam and Eve failed to fulfill.

God's Kingdom Through Us

Understanding these truths allows us to see God's strategy of colonization and therefore understand God's purpose behind it. God is the King of all creation: Heaven, Earth, and Universe. Again, He created Earth to be a colony of the Kingdom of Heaven. So, mankind was made to rule, to bring the dominion of His Kingdom on Earth.

The Kingdom of God is the only kingdom in which every member is part of the royal family-- sons and daughters of the King. It is a country, a nation, and a government all rolled into one. And we are its citizens. Consider Peter's revelation in 1 Peter 2:9: "You are a chosen race, a royal priesthood, a holy nation, a people for God's possession so that you may proclaim the excellencies of Him who called you out of darkness into His marvelous light."

As noted, Isaiah 9:6 says that Jesus carries the government on His shoulders, and there will be no end to the propagation of that government and His peace. Now comes the tie-in to the word Jesus used for His body, His Ekklesia, His Church. We have governmental authority on Earth to bring the nature and culture of the Kingdom of God to this planet and people.

We, like the Roman Senate, are appointed by the true Emperor and King, knowing His heart and His agenda, called and mandated to legislate the King's business on the earth with the authority that He possesses and has shared with us. The same infectious Kingdom atmosphere manifested by Jesus on the earth that drew so many to Him, is the same atmosphere we are called to manifest in our own lives today.

The Hebrew word for glory, Kabod, is used to describe the weight that produces the imprint or essence of God. It, in turn, describes the manifest culture of God's Kingdom. In Colossians 1, Paul described this indwelling glory as the very mystery of God: "That is, the mystery which has been hidden from the past ages and generations, but has now been manifested to His saints, to whom God willed to make known what is the riches of the glory of this mystery among the Gentiles, which is Christ in you, the hope of glory" (Colossians 1:26-27 NASB). This glory is the call and purpose of the Ekklesia that Jesus describes: to carry by His Spirit the who and how of God in us and to imprint the essence of God on the earth and all of creation.

Dominion: Birthright of the Sons of God

Let's now look at this word dominion from our Genesis 1:26 mandate, as it is key to finding God's purpose and man's assignment in that purpose. Myles Munroe in his book, *Rediscovering the Kingdom*, gives this derivation of the word dominion:

"The words dominion or rule are synonymous and derive their meanings from the same root words. The Hebrew words from which the concept of kingdom dominion comes are rendered mashal, mamlakah, and malkut; and the Greek derivative is the word basileia. The definition of these words includes 'to rule,' 'sovereignty,' 'to reign,' 'kingdom,' 'to master,' 'to be king,' 'royal rule,' and 'kingly.' The term mamlakah also signifies the area and the people that constitute a 'kingdom.'

"Therefore the definition of dominion can be crafted in the following way: 'To be given dominion means to be established as a sovereign, kingly ruler, master, governor, responsible for reigning over a designated territory, with the inherent authority to represent and embody as a symbol, the territory, resources, and all that constitutes that kingdom'" (Munroe 2010, 31-32).

Dominion Over Darkness
 "Rule" brings the concept of justice and rightness on the earth by way of destroying the works of the inferior, counterfeit kingdom of darkness. In countless instances, Jesus ruled over sickness to dispel the dominion of darkness. In Luke 13:11-13, Jesus exercised this kingly dominion of His Father to set free a woman who was bound by Satan for years, bringing her true justice. In John 5, Jesus heals a man who had been ill for 38 years. He explains in verse 17, "My Father is working until now, and I Myself am working." He went on to say that the Son did nothing on His own but only did what He sees the Father doing! This is revolutionary if we fully grasp what Jesus reveals here. First, the Father is always working; He is always doing more than we notice! And second, Jesus reveals that in Heaven, God the King has total dominion over the works of darkness in Heaven, so He brings that dominion through Jesus, mirroring it on the earth! If we can see the connection we have through the Spirit of God in us to what is in Heaven, we will exercise more and more the rule of God on the earth, and that is what brings true justice.

Stewarding God's Resources
 The word "manage" brings in the concept of stewardship -- the stewarding of all the resources God has placed on the earth. We have to understand how important management is in God's Kingdom. God will not release more resources unless He sees management in place. In Genesis 2:5, we see this concept; "Now no shrub of the field was yet in the earth, and no plant of the field had yet sprouted. For the Lord, God had not

sent rain upon the earth, and there was no man to cultivate the ground" (NASB).

God withheld the rain until He placed mankind in the garden to manage and cultivate the ground, which shows this aspect of dominion. Since dominion brings an increase in the productive management of God's Earth and resources, we can see our dominion is essential in God's economy.

How we manage what God has given us sets the tone for His release of more to us. We get more of what we manage well, but we lose what we do not manage well. For example, you are to manage and cultivate your marriage or possibly lose it. You are to cultivate and manage your money to grow it for Kingdom use or lose it. You are to cultivate and manage all your resources in a way that brings God's dominion and increase. The reward of management is behind the scripture in Matthew 13:12, "Whoever has will be given more, and he will have an abundance."

This leads us to another meaning of dominion, "to master." This meaning is tied into seeing God's Kingdom influence come more and more in the realms of the seven mountains: government, media, arts and entertainment, business, education, religion, and family. "To master" indicates we are to recognize the gifts God has uniquely given us for our specific assignment of bringing the ways of Heaven to Earth. And with this discovery, we are to master *our gifts* so that they *bring the glory and culture of God* into our specific assignment regardless of our "mountain" or area of influence. This is the opposite of being a jack-of-all-trades. We are called to master the gifts God has given us.

Think of dominion this way: *God has commissioned you to rule and reign over a designated territory of your gifting, with the inherent authority to embody, as a representative, the solutions, resources, and all that constitutes the Kingdom of God in your earthly assignment.*

This is the beauty of the dominion mandate given to mankind!

Ekklesia and God's Government

An Unshakeable Foundation
  The power of Ekklesia resides in the authority given to the body of Christ. He is our rock and foundation. The rock that Jesus says His Church will be built on in Matthew 16:18 is the same rock in Daniel 2:35, the great boulder that destroys all of the other kingdoms of the world and then grows and grows and grows until it fills the whole earth.
  This rock is the Kingdom of God; Ekklesia is built upon the King and His Kingdom-- which cannot fail, cannot be defeated and will never be stopped by the gates of Hades. Satan showed Jesus the counterfeit world systems during the temptation described in Luke 4:5. One concept of Hades-- full of fire and brimstone-- can make Hades feel far away; however, considering the Luke 4 passage, gates of Hades are much more tangible and present-- it includes inferior world systems and spiritual principalities which contradict the power and purpose of the Kingdom of God. Satan stole the true authority God gave mankind and has permeated the cultures of Earth with a counterfeit influence that kills,

steals, and destroys. The good news is that Jesus won that authority back and has restored us to the place of Kingdom rule and dominion to displace this inferior influence.

Paul highlights this restoration back to God's Kingdom when he declared in Colossians 1:13 that God's Ekklesia has been taken OUT of the domain of darkness and transferred INTO the light of the Kingdom of His beloved Son, Jesus!

God Rules Inside, Then Outside

The purpose of Ekklesia is to carry out the expansion of God's government on the earth. The rule of God that is within us grows and expands until it can exercise true and right dominion on the outside in the world. This growing rule of God highlights the powerful ongoing process of the Holy Spirit, discipling and transforming believers into the image of Jesus Christ. This discipleship is best walked out in these close relational communities of Ekklesia.

We were created by God to be ruled on the inside by His invisible spirit, and the more there is Kingdom rule on the inside, the less government we need on the outside. This was God's plan from the beginning. He was to be the king although He would rule ultimately through His sons and daughters. When Israel came out of slavery and journeyed toward the Promised Land, God told Moses that they would be a kingdom of priests to Him and that He would be their ruler. But the Israelites would not agree to it and told Moses to go and talk to God instead. Eventually, they asked for a king, a visible king like the other nations, and rejected God's rulership. Israel feared the closeness of such a powerful God, the intimacy with Him, and felt more comfortable with an exterior king or system of rules.

If the Israelites had chosen to allow deep intimacy with God to rule over their hearts and minds, they would not have needed a human king. Today, we can choose to be ruled by the wisdom of His Word, the power of His spirit and our connection to His heart.

Principles of Ekklesia

A Living Organism

The same principle of an inside rule that manifests on the outside applies to Ekklesia. Ekklesia meets and gathers on the inside and then displays the rule of God on the outside in culture. Think about it this way: Ekklesia breathes in and out as a living organism.

So first, Ekklesia *breathes in* connection with the Holy Spirit and each other as the powerful body of Christ. As the Ekklesia gathers, Kingdom assignments and struggles are shared and breakthroughs are prayed for. Ekklesia, then fortified by the promises of God to act on the agreement of His people, presses in together to secure ground for the Kingdom of Heaven. This is what Matthew 11:12 declares, "From the days of John the Baptist until now the kingdom of heaven suffers violence, and violent men take it by force" (Matthew 11:12, NASB).

Then through targeted agreement in prayer and declarations, God's provision, protection, and purpose are released to secure breakthrough and see ground taken for the Kingdom.

Ekklesia then *breathes out*-- going out to the marketplace, businesses, schools, governments, arts, and entertainment centers to bring the creativity, wisdom and insight of God, to show others the functionality of God. To show His solutions through us: solutions that work well and display His glory.

Just as a training athlete breathes deeper and stronger through practice, so the Ekklesia grows in power and focus. This breathing in and breathing out brings a greater impact of God's will in our cities, vocations, neighborhoods, schools, and homes. At this point I want to make a clear distinction between God's purpose and our assignments.

Purpose vs. Assignment

Too often, we confuse purpose and assignment. The clear purpose of God is to bring His kingdom on the earth through His sons and daughters. Once we get that deep in us, we can then find our place-- our unique assignment in His purpose. Too often, believers have been encouraged to "find their unique purpose" when they need to find their unique assignment within God's purpose.

A story told by Mario Murillo explains this well:

The Recruit on the Marine Base

"Imagine a young recruit in the Marines. On the first day of boot camp, he is standing at attention, and his drill sergeant barks a question at him, 'Why did you join the Marines?'

Imagine the young nob recruit answering him, 'To find my purpose, Sir!' About three days later, when the swelling in his eyes and the ringing in his ears subsided, he can still hear the Sergeant yelling, 'You have no Purpose! Only the Corps has a Purpose! What you have is an Assignment!'" (Murillo, 116).

Jesus and the Father have the purpose. You, my friend, have an assignment inside that purpose. God's will, then, for us, is found in who and how God made us for our assignment. It is amazing but once we see and lock into God's purpose of bringing the culture of Heaven on Earth, it is easier to press into our unique assignment. First, what do we love? What has been dropped deeply in us that draws our attention? Here is a clue: *where your heart is, there is your treasure.*

Second, look for patterns in the gifts, talents, and passions God has given you. There, your unique assignments will begin to emerge. Though it may take years to fully manifest, God's unique workmanship will continue to unfold before you. These gifts will help you connect with other believers who were created to influence the same or similar aspects of society. This is part of developing an Ekklesia and will be mentioned later in the book.

As believers begin to champion each other in our earthly assignments-- walking arm in arm, giving and receiving prophetic encouragement-- each one is propelled forward in a specific area of influence and ultimately advances the Kingdom of God. Believers participating as Ekklesia can't wait to connect to others who are like-minded with the desire to breathe in our shared Kingdom life and be refueled, recharged and refocused-- ready to step into the world and bring the who and how of God, the culture of His Kingdom in their world.

Jacob's Vision of the Ladder

Jacob's vision in Genesis 28:12-17 is a prophetic picture of the conduit of the Ekklesia bringing Heaven on Earth. Jacob saw a ladder on the earth reaching to Heaven with angels ascending and descending. Then

Jacob got the revelation in verse 17, "This is none other than the house of God, the gate of heaven." Jesus then tied this revelation to himself in John 1:51, saying, "Truly, truly I say to you, you will see the heavens opened and the angels of God ascending and descending on the Son of Man" (John 1:51, NASB). Jesus was the very conduit of Heaven when He was here, opening Heaven when He was baptized, then bringing the reality of Heaven on Earth as He released the love, healing, freedom, and forgiveness of God here in our midst.

Jesus was the second Adam, restoring the prototype of what mankind was created for: the house, the gate, and conduit of God's Kingdom and will on Earth! In Romans 8:29, Paul reinforces the idea of Jesus as the firstborn among many to follow, and he encourages all believers in 1 Corinthians 3:16 when he says, "Do you not know that you are the very house (temple) of God and that the Spirit of God dwells in you?" (NASB).

Expansion: Ekklesia and Kingdom

As I write this, we are in a global time-out caused by Covid-19. Large gatherings are prohibited, so "church" as we have known it is now online both for weekend messages from pastors and small groups. They continue to connect on Zoom and other video conferencing platforms. I believe that Isaiah 43:18-19 speaks clearly to this time as Isaiah encouraged us from the Lord, "Do not call to mind the former things, or ponder things of the past. Behold, I will do something new, now it will spring forth; Will you not be aware of it?" (Isaiah 43:18-19, NASB). We are certainly in a new thing!

How Ekklesia will meet has probably changed forever, but this invites us to a whole new world where believers meet in smaller but more effective and powerful units. This is starting to feel like the Ekklesia that Jesus envisioned, where His body meets and breathes in the Holy Spirit in both strategy and empowerment. His body then goes forth to breathe out the prayer of Jesus of bringing Heaven on Earth in our assignments. When Ekklesia comes together in agreement, Jesus is in the midst of us as we legislate for His Kingdom to manifest, believing His promise of Matthew 18:19, "Again I say to you, if two of you agree on earth about anything that they may ask, it shall be done for them by my Father who is in Heaven!" (Matthew 18:19, NASB).

As we have noted earlier, when the Ekklesia gathers together in these small, powerful groups, we legislate Kingdom business as it ought to be on the earth through prayers of agreement. These prayers of agreement are aimed especially for our country, our families and our unique assignments. We realize the results of prayers of agreement more and more as we possess the Kingdom of God and all of His sovereignty, power and greatness spoken of in Daniel 7:27, "Then the sovereignty, the dominion and the greatness of all the kingdoms under the whole heaven will be given to the people of the saints of the Highest One; His kingdom will be an everlasting kingdom, and all the dominions will serve and obey Him" (NASB).

The next step of breathing out involves Ekklesia naturally moving into their places of influence. Here the prayers of agreement are given feet and walked out as we step into real-life situations, bringing His ways, His nature, His principles, His keys and His functionality into all aspects of society.

This is what, beginning with Lance Wallnau and Johnny Enlow, is now referred to as the seven mountain mandate (see item #4 below in the

Guidelines): the Ekklesia operates in agreement together, contending for a breakthrough in each other's lives, areas of influence and vocations. Then, as the members of the group go out into society, they begin to see the Kingdom of God become real in their lives and the lives of those whom they love and influence.

Mankind, without the influence of God's Spirit, has failed to come close to what God intended for us in union with Him. But His Kingdom, ruled by the law of love, is exactly what everyone would want if they could experience it in all of its fullness: experiencing rightness, justice, peace, joy, liberty, dreams fulfilled, freedom of expression and relational harmony.

Can You See it? Can You Envision it?

I know this will sound utopian, but can you see an Earth where everyone is ruled on the inside by the King and His Kingdom: no murders, no lying, no stealing, no adultery, no greed, only the rightness, peace and joy of God's Kingdom?

God's plan flows out of His purpose. The plan of God will unfold and succeed as He continues to gather, build, and mobilize His Ekklesia on Earth. In Romans, Paul explains that this is what the world is longing for: "...the anxious longing of the creation waits eagerly for the revealing of the sons (and daughters) of God...that the creation itself will be set free from its slavery to corruption into the freedom of the glory of the children of God." (Romans 8:19, 21, NASB).

Awake sons and daughters of God! This is where God is heading, and we are being summoned to accept our assignment: His rule and His government in us to bring the freedom and the glory of the culture of Heaven on the earth in our area of influence.

Ekklesia: A Practical Overview

First and foremost, as sons and daughters of the King, we must each make the choice to allow the rulership of God to be first in our lives and hearts, which means we engage in the process of receiving Jesus Christ to be King and Lord. This first key step will work only as well, or as completely, as the transformation takes place within each believer. Paul gives us the call in Philippians 2 to "work out your salvation with fear and trembling" but he adds the empowerment for that: "for it is God who is at work in you, both to will and to work for His good pleasure" (Philippians 2:12b-13). I want to make it clear that this is the most transforming and liberating process ever; it is not a drudgery! Seek first the kingdom of God and His righteousness, and all these other things will be added unto us! (Matthew 6:33).

When we, as citizens of the Kingdom of God, step fully into our authority and understanding of the role of bringing kingdom dominion on the earth in every segment of life and culture, we will then be drawn together by the Holy Spirit to do Kingdom business. Like the Roman citizens who were in the Senate, appointed by the Emperor because they knew him and knew his agenda, so we are chosen by our King and are brought together by the Holy Spirit in a way that is strategic in maximizing His Kingdom advancement. I foresee that these groups of Ekklesia will be more and more strategically connected in assignments that relate to the seven mountains of culture. As Ekklesia groups begin to take root, they will learn how to operate together as citizens who are agreeing and legislating God's government around them in their world. I can see these groups will become more specialized as they take new ground and as they target cultural mountains.

Ekklesia groups do not have to be made up of many people, probably somewhere between 3 and 12. It is key that we pray and ask God to direct us to who we are to be connected to as we are going to be intimately involved in each other's lives in such a way that we know each other's assignments, prophetic words and dreams that God has placed over our lives. We will know each other's life verses and callings, and we will agree with Him and see each other advance the Kingdom and destroy the works of the enemy. In this way, there can be strong total agreement: where two or three agree it shall be done. So Ekklesia groups are meant to be large enough to impact a group of people, but small enough so that individual impact can happen as well. Glory-- kabod, the weightiness or heaviness that makes an impact or an imprint, will begin to mark the circumstances and people in the lives of each Ekklesia. The next step is that the growing work of the Ekklesia, full of God's glory, heaviness and imprint, increasingly makes a difference for the advancing of the Kingdom in the surrounding culture.

Ekklesia manifests the glory of God in aspects of the secular, or outside world. As members of Ekklesia gather in Kingdom authority, God's glory as culture will manifest on the outside in their vocations, recreation, relationships, and all other aspects of life. We showcase not only WHO God is but HOW He operates. In our **government** we showcase the *King*; in **business**, we showcase the *Provider*; in our **arts and entertainment** we showcase the *Creator*; in **education**, we showcase the *Teacher*; in **media and information** we showcase *His goodness*; in **science**, we showcase *His intelligent design*; in **medicine**, we showcase the *Healer*; in **families**, we showcase the *Father's love*; and of course in the **church**, we mirror the *Redeemer*. This is the seven mountain mandate!

Conclusion

As we conclude, I want to again have us consider the word *glory*. Maybe you have heard the phrase, "The glory of Rome." Rome's glory was the manifestation of its culture carried out through the entire empire. The envoys took Roman culture to the outer reaches of the realm so that when the emperor visited, it would feel like home. The same is true for God and His Kingdom. His glory manifested is the culture of His Kingdom. We can now see how the promise of Habakkuk 2:14, "For the earth will be filled with the knowledge of the glory of the Lord, as the waters cover the sea," will be fulfilled! (Habakkuk 2:14, NASB).

This will happen step by step, inch by inch, as the true church shows up in the world and pushes aside the inferior works of the counterfeit kingdom of darkness and instead manifests the true knowledge of the Kingdom of God on Earth. Remember how the Ekklesia in Matthew 16:18 will overcome the gates of Hades? Through proximity, being near to these gates, we have a strategic position to overcome and replace these inferior systems. Proximity is power. That is why scripture is clear; we are to be IN the world and not OF it. So Jesus has given us a calling and the power, authority and wisdom to go in and push back this system ruled by darkness. As we walk in His authority and power, we will bring the true light and knowledge of how this earth was created to operate and mirror Heaven in nature and functionality; both the WHO and the HOW of God.

So my final encouragement is: find your Ekklesia. Start meeting and breathing in together the strategy and power of the Holy Spirit for your Kingdom assignments. Then breathe out into your world the very culture and reality of Heaven until we start seeing more of the Kingdom come and the will of Father God be done on Earth.

My prayer is Philippians 2:13, that you would know who you are because you know who God is and that He is in you to will and act according to His good pleasure and purpose!

Ekklesia Field Guide

Designed to be used along with the e-book *Ekklesia: Empowered and Deployed*, this Field Guide provides practical help for establishing an Ekklesia. *Ekklesia: Empowered and Deployed* gives a more thorough biblical foundation for the formation and deployment of these Ekklesia units.

What is Ekklesia?

Ekklesia is a group of believers gathered in the name of Jesus Christ to conduct His Kingdom's governmental business in our assignments. Most of us are used to what the modern church has called small groups: 10 to maybe 15 people meeting together regularly to support each other in our Christian walk, discussing the weekly sermon or Bible study. These have been great support groups. I have been involved with small groups for at least 40 years with my wife Libby, and I've always been in some sort of small group of Christians meeting monthly. Small groups, providing prayer, discipleship and emotional support in times of need, are not to be discounted; they have certainly helped many believers to make it through tough times. But Ekklesia is different in that the Commander's intent of bringing the reality of the Kingdom of Heaven to earth in our assignment remains our clear focus and aim.

The difference in typical small groups and what I am experiencing with Ekklesia is that Ekklesia focuses on advancing the Kingdom's agenda of Heaven on the earth. It acknowledges that every believer has an assignment for colonizing the earth with Heaven. That assignment stems from the way God has wired believers in their passions, gifts, and personality, placing them where they function best.

Why Ekklesia?
   Ekklesia is the transformational entity that Jesus said He would build with the sons and daughters of God, the sons and daughters of His Kingdom. The world needs Ekklesia! The world needs us to show up! The world needs you to show up! The world needs you to show up in your assignment and your passion and your gifts filled with God, with the CCC of God in you:
the constant communication and connection restored through Jesus. This restoration means you are now co-regents-- you are now a true ambassador of the nation of the Kingdom of God. Will you bring the government of God upon your shoulders in your world? Remember, you are the body of Christ! Christ's government will know no limit, and there will be no limit to His peace!
   Why Ekklesia? Because Romans 8:21 says, the earth is groaning in travail for the revealing of the glory of the sons of God! Creation groans to see the freedom and liberty His sons and daughters demonstrate and manifest on the earth: freedom and liberty in business, in government, in education and entertainment and sports, in media and family. God is going to raise up groups of 3-12 who meet breathing IN the empowerment, the healing, the strategy and wisdom of the Holy Spirit together, and then breathing OUT through their unique assignments. God's purpose is bringing the reality of Heaven on the ground, for all.

Guidelines of Ekklesia

Knowing your assignment is different than knowing your purpose, but this distinction is powerful. *A big part of the Ekklesia breathing out God's Kingdom culture on Earth is believers finding their assignment in His purpose.* Too often, we confuse purpose and assignment. God does everything with purpose. He is the designer of designers. Even the color of a particular flower draws the right bee to pollinate that flower properly.

So God is a God of purpose. He was purposeful in creating mankind. God created Earth and then created mankind connected to His Spirit and heart to colonize earth with the Kingdom of Heaven's culture. Adam and Eve had the only thing that would make this possible: constant communication and connection! CCC! Jesus repeated God's purpose when He taught His disciples how to pray: "Your Kingdom come and your will be done, on Earth as it is in heaven!" Once we get God's purpose deep IN us, we then find our place, our assignment in that purpose.

Perhaps you have always had a love for cooking, horseback riding, or engineering: God doesn't want you to go door to door with salvation tracks; He wants to help you reveal His glory in the things you already love! You don't need to spend years trying to discover what God created you to do; you need to know who you are in connection to Him! When someone tastes your latest dish, experiences the joy of being one with nature, or sees your latest solution to a company problem-- you are displaying God's glory and are working in your assignment. God will give you opportunities to share with others that He is the King of creativity, nature, and even product design! Their hearts will be opened because they are experiencing the aspects of the Kingdom of God that you carry while you are doing what you already love to do!

Recently, I was in the dental office where I worked for a time, when the office manager, who had just returned from a battle with COVID-19, began to tell me about her lingering physical problems from the illness. As she told me about her discomforts, I asked-- right there in the office-- if I could pray for her healing. She agreed, and I prayed.

Pray for those who eat your meals to be healed and to feel the love of God! Ask to lay hands on your injured riding buddy and explain that Jesus is the healer. When your boss wants to talk to you about the brilliant solution you had to the company problem, tell him that you follow the God of solutions!

Guidelines and Practices of Ekklesia

The key components of Ekklesia are a small but focused group of believers (12 or less) that are called together by the Holy Spirit to convene and conduct Kingdom business in the assignments that God has given each one in the seven areas of cultural influence. We believe that God has given us abilities in our vocations and in our talents and gifts that bring us into arenas of culture to bring Kingdom Reality.

These mobile, micro-churches, or true Ekklesia, are believers that are locked together, pressing in and displacing the gates of hades populated by people who are under the influence of the lies of Satan. When Jesus used the word gate, it meant the place of influence in a city, so He was declaring that these gates influenced by hades would be displaced and replaced by His Ekklesia, bringing the very culture of Heaven here.

This gathering needs at least 2 or 3 intimate, powerful, loving relationships. Transparency and an authentic desire to grow more and more into the fullness of Christ creates a powerful environment for transformation. Knowledge of each other's assignments and support for one another becomes similar to the concept of warriors locking shields together to take ground for the Kingdom of God. They become a force multiplier together.

Daniel: An Example of Ekklesia

In Daniel 2, we see how Ekklesia can work to alter the destiny of people and nations. The chapter begins with King Nebuchadnezzar's terrifying dream. He demands that his magicians, conjurers, sorcerers and Chaldeans not only interpret the dream but also recount the dream to him. If they failed to do so, they would be torn limb from limb, and their houses made into rubbish heaps.

Daniel, being a leader of this group, went to the King and respectfully asked for time that he might declare both the dream and the interpretation to him. Daniel then went to his house and convened his Ekklesia that consisted of 3 Hebrew friends; they prayed and asked God for compassion concerning this request so they and their group would not be destroyed. God answered: He gave Daniel the dream and the interpretation, which led the King to declare,

"Surely your God is a God of gods and a Lord of kings and a revealer of mysteries since you have been able to reveal this mystery" (Daniel 2:47, NASB).

The King recognized that there was an invisible God who ruled the earth because he saw a physical Daniel who represented Him on Earth! Then the King promoted Daniel to be the ruler over the whole province of Babylon and chief prefect over all the wise men of Babylon. So here you see clearly the Ekklesia of God convene and legislate God's will on the earth and bring solutions that save people's lives and bring glory to God. That is the work of Ekklesia!

Ekklesia in Action

Dentistry Ekklesia Sample

As a dentist, my Ekklesia knows all about what is happening in our office and where prayer and agreement are needed to bring more of the atmosphere of God's presence. At work recently, I felt a nudge to pray for a patient, sensing that God had ministry He had prepared for her. Knowing that I would see this patient several times over a short period of time, I asked my Ekklesia to pray for the right words and the right opportunity to share with her. Well, prayers were answered! The door of opportunity opened, and I was able to share and pray with her and knew God's kingdom had advanced in her heart!

Geographic Ekklesia Sample

A neighborhood Ekklesia can be powerful as believers meet to see God's Kingdom come and advance in their geographic assignment. As the Ekklesia meet, they are targeting prayer needs of neighbors, seeing folks come to Christ, illnesses healed, finances restored, and relationships healed. In this group, maturity, trust, and confidentiality are paramount as people's lives are lifted up for healing and not for gossip. That is another reason why the Holy Spirit initiates Ekklesia formation, so those connected are fitted and prepared by the Holy Spirit for their assignment.

Government Ekklesia Scenario
   Jacob has a passion for politics. Growing up, he was drawn to the Constitution's intricacies and was grieved by the corruption that appeared so evident in the various political parties. Jacob met Jim at a pick-up soccer game and discovered that Jim, too, had a passion for seeing a change in politics.
   They decided to take action and research local political organizations. Jacob joined one, and Jim joined another. During an event hosted by these two groups, they met Meg and Amanda. Meg and Amanda believed God called them to join an organization to be a positive Christian influence and to pray for the leadership. Amanda felt God calling her to run for one of the leadership positions and shared this with Meg, Jim, and Jacob over dinner.
   Jacob saw the common passion between these new friends. He suggested they get together twice a month to intentionally pray and support one another as they take ground in their respective organizations-- for the good of the community. They came together and supported Amanda as she ran for the leadership position, praying for her and giving her wisdom, support, and guidance.
   Jim, inspired by Amanda's boldness, decided to run for a local political office to bring positive change there as well. Meg felt the Lord lead her to speak life into a new friend in the political organization of which she and Amanda are members. This new-comer was Buddhist, but Meg saw that God was giving this person creative ideas and solutions for the organization. With prayer and support from her Ekklesia, she approached the new-comer and asked

if she could share a prophetic word of encouragement from the Lord. Because of Meg's genuine nature, the new-comer trusted her and allowed her to speak into her life.

The group continues to meet regularly to pray for and support each other as they influence the mountain they are drawn to for the Kingdom of God.

Arts and Entertainment Ekklesia Scenario

Nylejiah and Simon met at a local coffee shop. A conversation that began over coffee preferences led to the realization that they both worked in the entertainment industry and shared a belief in Jesus. Nylejiah, working as the director for a local theatre and Simon, growing as an aspiring film-maker, decided to get a few friends together for a brainstorming session.

At first, Nylejiah and Simon invited only two other friends, all with Christian beliefs. They met together for dinner and discussed the community in which they lived. They shared dreams for the theatre, for possible film venues, for actors, actresses, directors and playwrights they knew in common. Over second helpings of spaghetti, Jack and Alexandra opened up about their desire to start a theatre school for high school and college students in the area. They had never shared this dream out loud with anyone but each other. Together, the group decided to meet for dinner once a month. (Their schedules would not allow for more frequent meetings.) Nylejiah and Simon made it a point to reach out to those they had invited to the dinner and send messages of encouragement once per week to stay connected.

A little over a year later, Alexandra gave Simon an unexpected call a few days before the next scheduled dinner, "You won't believe what God is doing! I just ran into a director who is moving here from New York. Before I knew it, I was sharing my dreams for a local theatre school. He gave me his card and said he had a few friends who might be interested in investing once I get a plan together. Can you believe that? It's not a done deal, but woah! I never dreamed I would ever have the opportunity even to use the word investors!"

Simon relayed the information to Nylejiah, and they planned a special celebration in place of dinner that month. *It was time to help Alexandra make a plan for future investors!*

Notes for Getting Started

Your First Ekklesia Meeting

So, what about your first Ekklesia meeting? First, it is best to have someone lead and facilitate a group that is more than 2 or 3 people, and that role can be rotated. The first order of business in a new Ekklesia is to review the foundational truth that we were created to represent God and His heavenly government through exercising Kingdom dominion in the spheres of influence through the gifts and assignments we each have. Always the first order of business is to keep the Commander's intent in front of us that we are heavenly immigrants on the earth, bringing the will, mind, intent, and the purpose of the benevolent rule of God's Kingdom to the earth.

Then each person introduces who they are and starts to share where they are in their discovery of their assignment in God's purpose based on the passions and gifts He has placed in them along with their current sense of where He has placed them. As each person shares, the others listen and record the revelations they get about that person and their assignment.

This will be an ongoing process as God breathes His strategy and wisdom for each person, and breakthrough becomes a reality. After each person has shared, individuals can share verses in which new meaning has been revealed or previous understanding strengthened. The group then moves into worship that leads the group into agreement for breakthrough often with prophetic words of encouragement. We have found it is helpful to write out the prayer targets on a white board to help while we pray and also so these can be shared to the group for ongoing agreement between sessions.

The group then decides when and where to meet again. After the meeting, members go forth to breathe out the Kingdom of Heaven in their assignments. This breathing IN and OUT will get stronger and stronger as the group meets and presses in to grab hold of God's advancing Kingdom (see Matthew 11:12).

Common Issues and How to Solve Them

First, the Ekklesia unit needs to realize that Satan hates for powerful Ekklesia units to form, become, and do the one thing he hates the most: the Ekklesia of God overcoming the gates of hades in the world. So we need to be very aware that Satan's biggest weapon is accusing the people of God. He and his little imps will start whispering accusations and lies against each other right away. He will try to bring whatever lie he can bring to create distance and diminish the effectiveness of Ekklesia's powerful intent. Be on guard and watch for accusations and disunity to come from the enemy and destroy his work. And as 1 Peter 5:8 says, "Be of sober spirit, be on the alert. Your adversary, the devil, prowls around like a roaring lion, seeking someone to devour. But resist him, firm in your faith."

Second, in any warfare that comes with the advancement of the Kingdom, people get tired and wounded. The group must navigate this correctly, so that the Commander's intent and purpose stay clear and focused while caring and healing are brought to those who need ministry. This ministry can be given during the meeting, and in between, assuring that the purpose of God to bring the reality of His Kingdom in our world remains the focus. I believe that keeping the Commander's intent clear creates the best atmosphere for healing and restoration as we are being restored with the Father's best destiny in our hearts for each other.

Q: What happens if someone wants to leave the Ekklesia because he or she feels called to a different area of influence or group?

A: That is precisely what we expect to happen as believers grow in the practice of breathing in and out in Ekklesia and gain more clarity of their assignment! As groups grow in influence, more people will look for folks in their assignment area or 7 Mountain arena.

Q: What if I don't feel called to change government or education or another larger area of influence, but I want to see my children or family strengthened? Can I lead an Ekklesia that is not explicitly included in the "7 Mountain Mandate?"

A: Sure! Ekklesia supports where God has you right now with the focus of bringing Heaven's influence and seeing the will of God being done. It can be a group that is focused on influencing the relationships in their lives. Meeting every two weeks and just bringing the prayer focus to these relationships will bring advancement in the Kingdom of God coming in these relationships. The key again is agreeing to the purpose of God to colonize the earth with Heaven everywhere God has us! We live and move and have our being in Him, the King!

Q: I'm loving this Ekklesia concept, Ron. So, let's say I start an Ekklesia. I can totally stop going to my regular church, right? An Ekklesia is essentially the local micro-church. What is the point of attending a Sunday service if I have a strong Ekklesia?

A: Of course, you do not have to stop attending the larger meetings. The key here is that there is a different focus and purpose for each of these gatherings that has to be realized now that we know what Jesus was aiming for when He declared He would build His ecclesia and the gates of hades would not prevail against it. Being in the midst of Covid-19, we have already begun to see smaller gatherings online and together in homes. As we noted before, there is a corporate presence of God and the voice of leadership that has brought tangible value to larger group worship and teaching that is hard to reproduce in the small groups. Many are also beginning to sense that the larger church gatherings will certainly be less strategic in getting believers activated into their assignment on the ground in the Big Purpose of God, our King. Believers are starting to understand that they must become the salt of the earth and the light of the world in culture to reform culture. Bill Johnson once said revival without reformation is no revival at all. So what is the best vehicle to do that in a consistent, focused way? The way Jesus described Ekklesia! The larger meeting is now icing on the cake, but the Ekklesia gathering is where the transformational entity Jesus called for can be experienced and walked out.

Testimony

Here is a recent email received from one of our Ekklesia comrades:

"It's amazing that we, (Ekklesia), can change the course of a city by activating believers who will manifest the realities of Kingdom life in their areas of influence. It's fun and exciting to be able to see into the future as the light comes on with individuals who finally realize that they are capable of the miraculous, seeing them transformed with prayer and into a better understanding of who they are in Christ. And then stepping into being a part of Ekklesia that is taking ground. I've got so many things going through my head, but the one thing that stands out is the vision that we embrace when we get together at your house, Ron. Knowing that there are hungry people, hungry Christians that want more of God-- that consumes me at times-- just knowing that we are part of what God's church really is. It's not OK to be just OK. Time to destroy the sacred cows. Love you guys."

Conclusion

So there you have it. I hope both the book, *Ekklesia, Empowered and Deployed* and the Field Guide have helped you see the simple strategy of Ekklesia that Jesus revealed to change and transform this world.

My final prayer is that of Paul's from Ephesians 1 beginning with verse 17, "that the God of our Lord Jesus Christ, the Father of Glory, may give to you a spirit of wisdom and revelation in the knowledge of Him. I pray that the eyes of your heart may be enlightened, so that you will know what is the hope of His calling, what are the riches of the glory of His inheritance in the saints, and what is a surpassing greatness of His power toward us who believe" (Ephesians 1:17-19a NASB).

Ekklesia, with God in us, let's go transform our world!

Text References

Munroe, Myles. *Rediscovering the Kingdom*. Pennsylvania: Destiny Image Publishers, Inc., 2010.

Murillo, Mario. *Vessels of Fire and Glory*. Pennsylvania: Destiny Image Publishers, Inc., 2020.

Strong's Exhaustive Concordance: New American Standard Bible. 1995. Updated ed. La Habra: Lockman Foundation. http://www.biblestudytools.com/concordances/strongs-exhaustive-concordance/.

A Note Regarding Scripture References

Unless otherwise noted, scriptural quotations are from the NEW AMERICAN STANDARD BIBLE copyright @ 1960,1962,1963,1968,1971,1972,1973,1975,1977, 1995 by the Lockman Foundation. Used by permission. Emphasis within Scriptural quotations is the author's own.

A Note Regarding the Field Guide

Short selections of the Field Guide including the Government Ekklesia Scenario and the Arts and Entertainment Ekklesia Scenario were written and contributed by Ashley E. Johnson.

Resources for Further Study

Ekklesia by Ed Silvoso
The Seven Mountain Prophecy by Johnny Enlow
Invading Babylon by Lance Wallnau and Bill Johnson